NASCAR RACERS™

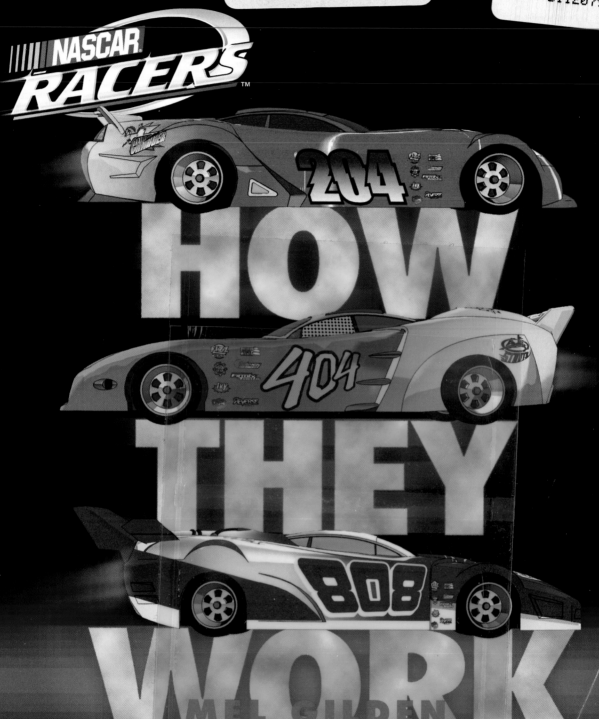

HOW THEY WORK

MEL GILDEN

HarperEntertainment
An Imprint of HarperCollinsPublishers

Collect all these awesome NASCAR Racers books!

NASCAR Racers: Official Owner's Manual

NASCAR Racers #1: The Fast Lane

NASCAR Racers #2: Taking the Lead

And coming in July 2000

NASCAR Racers #3: Tundra 2000

HarperEntertainment books may be purchased for educational, business, or sales promotional use. For information, please write to Special Markets Department, HarperCollins Publishers Inc., 10 East 53rd Street, New York, NY 10022.

Designed by Jeannette Jacobs

ISBN 0-06-107182-X

04 03 02 01 00 10 9 8 7 6 5 4 3 2 1

CHAPTER ONE
RACING RULES

WELCOME TO THE NASCAR UNLIMITED DIVISION,
where cars and drivers do the impossible! Unlimited Division
cars use cutting-edge equipment at unheard-of speeds—a
combination that is both incredibly exciting and incredibly dangerous. It takes knowledgeable, highly skilled drivers and pit crews
to handle cars like these.

One can't understand the machinery of the NASCAR Unlimited
Division without understanding the Unlimited Division itself.
Founded to test the latest in cutting-edge automotive technology,
the Unlimited Division is the most thrilling form of auto racing
ever created. Long before each season begins, every team is
told what off-road courses and superspeedway tracks they will

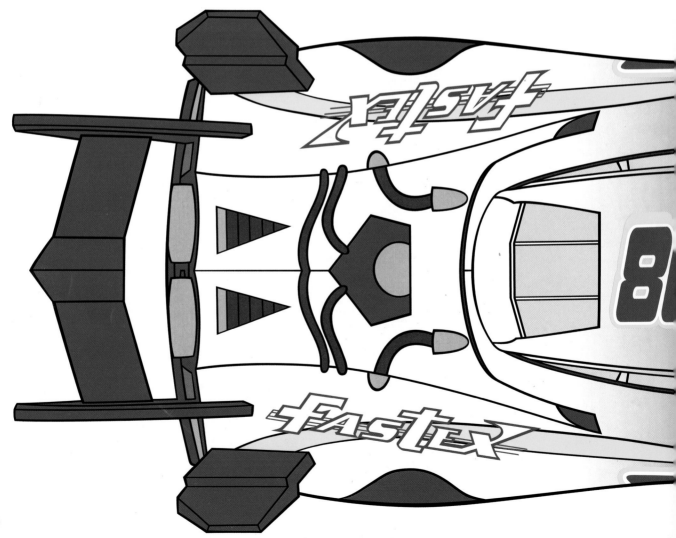

All cars are equipped with a "place sensor" that determines the order of finishers in a race. This technology is based on the same "electric eye" mechanism that automatically opens and closes your local supermarket's doors!

face. Every car is allowed the same range of capabilities. This means that—in theory—all of the Unlimited Division cars could have been created identically, able to perform the same amazing stunts and ready to handle any sort of off-road challenge. However, the more equipment and capabilities the cars have, the heavier they become. That makes the cars slower and

causes them to use more fuel. As everyone knows, slow cars don't win races, so the engineers and mechanics of each team have incorporated only those features that they feel are *most* likely to help a driver win. In addition, each car is designed with details to fit the special needs and talents of the driver and the specific requirements of each course. This means that every Unlimited Division driver has a unique car—one that is perfect for him or her alone. For example, Douglas "Duck" Dunaka, Fastex crew chief, helped equip Steve "Flyer" Sharp's car with wing-like attachments to play off of Flyer's training as an Air Force pilot. Flyer's car was later outfitted with a special buzz saw mechanism for an off-road course through the jungle. However, no matter what special equipment Unlimited Division cars carry, they must fit within certain set Division guidelines.

Unlimited Division races are either *speedway* or

off-road, and the technology developed for each race depends on whatever special challenges the course may hold. (Special equipment for specific races is discussed later in the book.) This experimental aspect of the Unlimited Division is what makes it so exciting. The "exotic" piece of equipment an Unlimited Division car uses may become standard equipment on all cars in the future. So look closely at the designs throughout the book—this is equipment you may use someday!

Since the inception of the Unlimited Division, there have been three instances in which drivers have contested the accuracy of finish line sensors' readings. In a case such as this, NASCAR Unlimited Division officials review the videotape of the race to verify the placement of the cars. In all cases, the accuracy of the sensors was reconfirmed.

CHAPTER TWO
THE TEAMS

I T TAKES INTELLIGENT, CAPABLE, AND FEARLESS drivers and crews to handle NASCAR Unlimited Division racers. Before becoming an official Unlimited Division team member, drivers and crew members must undergo strenuous testing—and they must continue training even after joining the team.

As stated in the previous chapter, Unlimited Division cars are designed with the drivers in mind. It would therefore be impossible to go into the details of the vehicles without first introducing their drivers and the support crew that designs and builds the cars. Once you are familiar with the personalities behind the designs, you will understand where some of their unique features come from.

We have chosen to focus on the top two teams in the Unlimited Division, Team Fastex and Team Rexcor, which employ very different racing styles.

THE DRIVERS
TEAM FASTEX

■ **Mark McCutchen**

Car Number: 204

AKA "Charger"

■ **Got his nickname:** Because he is likely to charge into a situation without thinking it through first.

Other information: Charger began racing go-carts at the age of six. Charger's family has been associated with NASCAR for three generations; racing is in his blood. His grandfather, Mack, raced

at Daytona, and won more than thirty races in his career. Charger's father, Junior, drove modifieds and sprint cars for many years, and had just begun racing for NASCAR when he died in a plane crash in the wilds of Alaska. Junior McCutchen also raced Car 204.

■ **Carlos Rey**

Car Number: 404

AKA "Stunts"

■ **Got his nickname:** Because he is a show-off and is likely to pull complicated, daring moves during a race.

Other information: When he was young, Stunts's parents left their teaching jobs to start their own business. Unfortunately, their business failed, and Stunts was raised in relative poverty. This has made him very eager to make a lot of money—and to make it soon. Stunts hopes to be a successful executive someday, and sees racing as a means of earning money to start his own business.

Stunts started out racing motorcycles, then moved to stock cars. He was setting records on the NASCAR Western Series tracks before he chose to move to the Unlimited Division. He often still drives as though his car is capable of the same sort of showy stunts as a motorcycle.

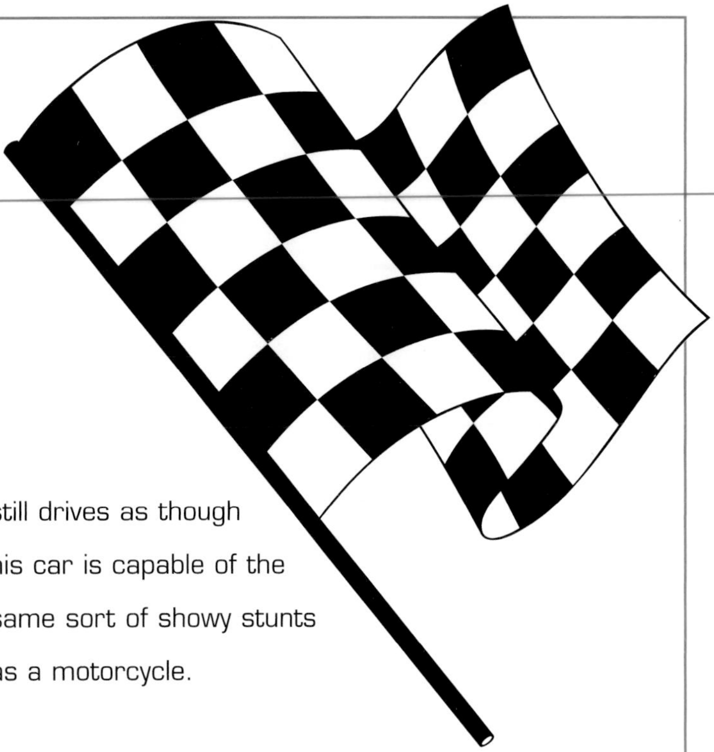

■ Steve Sharp

Car Number: 808

AKA "Flyer"

■ **Got his nickname:** Because he spent several years in the Air Force.

Other Information: Sharp's father served in the Air Force, and Sharp grew up on a dozen different military bases. While his father was a crew chief who repaired and maintained jet fighters, young Sharp dreamed of being a military flyer. He worked hard and was given an appointment to the Air Force Academy, where he took top

The test to become a **NASCAR Unlimited Division** driver is a grueling ten hours long, and is taken over two days.

Section A, given on the first day, is a written exam, covering the rules of Unlimited Division racing, safety features of the cars, and other information. Section B, given on the second day of testing, includes a virtual driving section and a section in which the drivers must rebuild part of an Unlimited Division racer engine.

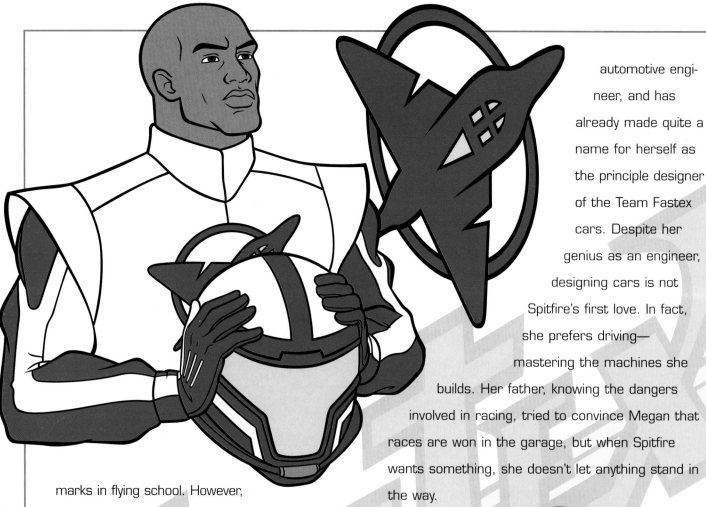

automotive engineer, and has already made quite a name for herself as the principle designer of the Team Fastex cars. Despite her genius as an engineer, designing cars is not Spitfire's first love. In fact, she prefers driving—mastering the machines she builds. Her father, knowing the dangers involved in racing, tried to convince Megan that races are won in the garage, but when Spitfire wants something, she doesn't let anything stand in the way.

marks in flying school. However, shortly after seeing action in an air strike against the biochemical weapons complex of a terrorist state, Sharp resigned from the Air Force. He gave no reason.

Soon after leaving the Air Force, Flyer joined the NASCAR Unlimited Division, and has quickly established himself as a top driver.

■ Megan Fassler

Car Number: 101

AKA "Spitfire"

■ **Got her nickname:** For her stubborn streak and sometimes harsh sense of humor.

Other information: As the daughter of Jack Fassler, the owner of Team Fastex, Megan grew up around cars and technology. Spitfire is a brilliant

TEAM REXCOR

■ Lyle Owens

Car Number: 606

AKA "The Collector"

■ **Got his nickname:** Because he often purposely causes accidents, and then collects parts from the cars he ruins as souvenirs.

Other information: Owens started out in the Unlimited Division driving for Team Fastex. However, when Jack Fassler discovered that Lyle was known as "The Collector"—and why—Lyle was fired. Soon thereafter, The Collector was hired to drive for Team Rexcor. In fact, The Collector had been working for Rexcor all along—as a spy.

The Collector is known to use a variety of dirty tricks to win races. He might swerve to cut off other drivers, or even bump them. One of his favorite dirty tricks is to rise into the air using his signature lever, and then come down hard on another car. However, it is possible for him to come down too hard. In that circumstance, his jet engines may suddenly close up into his car, causing it to spin out of control.

■ Hondo Hines

Car Number: 303

AKA "Specter"

■ **Got his nickname:** Because during a race he makes his move when it is least expected, appearing suddenly, like a ghost or specter.

11

Other Information: Many Unlimited Division drivers find Specter's driving style unnerving. He is a skillful driver who maintains an eerily threatening calm even during the most heated races. Like The Collector, Specter is known for dirty driving. When he makes a move against another driver, he strikes swiftly to wreck his competitor's vehicle.

■ Zorina

Car Number: 505
No Known Aliases.

Other Information: Zorina began her career in auto racing rather late, after she had already established herself as a model and body-builder. However, her phenomenal natural ability quickly qualified her to drive in NASCAR's most prestigious divisions. A thrill-seeker, Zorina was one of the first drivers to volunteer for the Unlimited Division.

Like her teammates, Zorina has been known to pull dirty tricks. In an attempt to bump competing cars off the track, Zorina may ram an opposing car from the side. She often uses the switch on her center console to

activate jets that push her against the opposing vehicle with tremendous force. However, this maneuver can backfire, as it may cause Zorina's car to spin out, requiring her to deploy her Rescue Racer.

■ Diesel Spitz

Car Number: 707

AKA "Junker"

■ Got his nickname: Because he has been known to wreck others' cars—as well as his own. (Note: Junker insists that his nickname should be pronounced "Yoonker." He claims that it is a family name, as he is descended from Prussian nobility. The truth of this statement has never been verified.)

Other Information: Junker was on his way to a championship in his first season of European Grand Prix racing when he was banned for flagrant rules violations. It is rumored that Junker moved to the United States because he was involved with illegal activities in Europe, and either the police were after him, or he had double-crossed some of his criminal associates.

Although Junker rarely finishes a race without wrecking his car, he always finishes, and often wins. On the rare occasions when his car finishes a race undamaged, Junker will work it over with a sledgehammer, just for luck. In fact, he often slams his car before a race, to psyche himself up for competition.

THE BOSSES
TEAM FASTEX

■ Jack Fassler

Jack Fassler is the founder, owner, and main force behind Fastex and Unlimited Division racing. He is responsible for the conception and building of New Motor City, home to the gigantic Motorsphere.

TEAM REXCOR

■ Garner Rexton

Garner Rexton is a genius who is out for revenge against Jack Fassler. Garner's company, Rexcor Corporation, is huge and powerful—and all of its resources are at the disposal of Team Rexcor.

THE CREWS
TEAM FASTEX

■ Douglas Dunaka

AKA "Duck"

■ Got his nickname: From his legendary ability to repair anything on a racecar using only the roll of duct tape that he always wears on his belt. (Duck refers to duct tape as "duck" tape.)

Other Information: At age forty-five, Duck Dunaka has had almost every job on a racing team from tire-changer to driver, and knows everything about cars and racing history. His crew includes mechanics, spotters, tire changers, and fuelers.

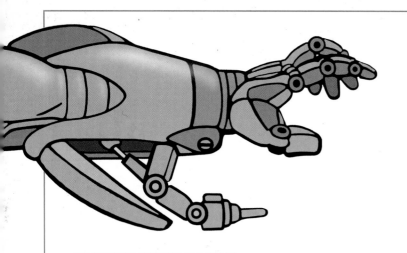

for something, he sees by means of a Terminator-style targeting device. His bionic parts contain hidden equipment. For example, his left arm contains a small blowtorch, and an electronic probe on a cable can be extended from his body. The wrist of his left hand hides a pneumatic wrench, which uses high-pressure blasts of air.

TEAM REXCOR

■ Spex

This part human, part cybernetic construct is Team Rexcor's Chief Engineer. Nobody knows his real name or who he was before Garner Rexton had him altered. He is very strong, has unnaturally sharp hearing, and speaks in a frightening electronic voice. When looking

CHAPTER THREE
THE CARS

IN NASCAR RACING THE CAR gets the most attention, and this is especially true of the amazing cars in the Unlimited Division. They have all the usual equipment—gauges, tires, seat belts, and so on. But they also have wings, jets, morphing tires, and cutting-edge computers. These are just a few of the features that make races in the Unlimited Division so exciting.

ENGINEERING DESIGN THEORY AND PRACTICE

Unlimited Division cars are constructed of strong but lightweight materials, such as special metals, plastics, rubbers, and ceramics. However, despite lightweight materials, Unlimited Division cars carry so much equipment that they are much heavier than conventional street vehicles.

Unlimited Division cars also have improved handling and safety features as well as engines with bigger displacements and higher compression. In addition, the carburetors employ the latest in forced-combustion technology. (Forced combustion is an updated method of turbocharging or supercharging, and adds performance to an engine by forcing air into the carburetor.) This means that Unlimited Division cars can reach speeds of up to 400 miles per hour on a superspeedway!

Small but sturdy onboard computers help control fuel mixtures and make minor adjustments in the engine as demands change. When a car is racing to pass another car it needs a richer fuel mixture—higher-octane gasoline—than it would if it was moving at a steady clip or idling. If the engine is getting hot, the car's computer increases the activity of the cooling system.

A regular **NASCAR** racing vehicle weighs approximately 3,500 pounds. But an Unlimited Division car with off-road equipment installed can weigh up to 5,600 pounds! Lighter cars can go faster than heavier ones, which is why Unlimited Division engineers are always looking for ways to cut the weight of their racecars, and, of course, to improve the performance of the incredibly powerful engines.

A carburetor mixes gas into air, creating the proper mixture to pass into the cylinders. The more air and fuel that a cylinder can take, the more power the cylinder will provide. The more power the cylinder provides, the faster the car can go. Forced combustion compresses a large air-and-fuel mix into Unlimited Division car cylinders, maximizing their power—and the car's speed.

SPECIAL FEATURES
AERODYNAMIC PANELS

Aerodynamic panels can be used as rudders to help steer the car, as braking mechanisms, or—when fully extended—as wings that allow the car to fly a few hundred feet. They activate automatically in emergency situations, or can be deployed by the driver when it could help win a race. It is possible to employ the wings for "jump passing" over another car. However, once the wheels leave the road, a car loses speed quickly unless the turbojet booster is engaged.

ROCKETS AND BOOSTERS

All boosters and jets must be used sparingly because they take a lot of fuel to run. A driver who uses them too often will find him- or herself stopping so often to refuel that he or she will lose any advantage gained. Also, there is always a chance that, as it lands, a flying car could become damaged by the track, or could accidentally bump another car on the road.

Turbojet boosters are small jet engines built into the car to give it greater speed when not touching the ground—such as when the aerodynamic panels are engaged—or when running on a slick surface such as ice. Front boosters can also aid in braking. This is very useful when attempting to stop a car going 400 miles per hour!

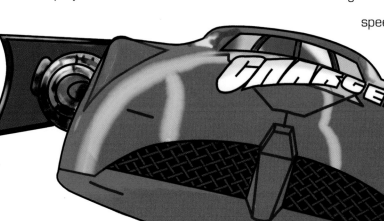

The combustion chamber in a turbojet engine takes in high-pressure air, combines the air with fuel, and burns the mixture. This means that turbojet boosters can get very—even dangerously—hot. How are they kept from overheating? Simple—turbojets are air-cooled. Only about a quarter of the air that is taken into the engine is burned in the combustion chamber. The remaining three-quarters passes around the combustion chamber, cooling it.

Control jets are smaller boosters located at the corners of each car. These can be used to enhance or regain control.

Rocket boosters are similar to turbojet boosters but are used to increase speed when the car is still on the ground. These can also be useful getting out of sandpits and other similar traps.

TEAM FASTEX CARS INTERIOR

The interior design of each Team Fastex car is the same. Most surfaces are black, but each driver has color accents that reflect the exterior of his or her car.

Charger's accents are red, Flyer's accents are blue, Stunts's are green, and Spitfire's are purple.

Note: there are no doors on Unlimited Division cars. The window on the driver's side is a

Unlimited Division cars with airborne capabilities, such as Flyer's, require special equipment to guide the wings. The part of the wing that can be adjusted to make the car fly up or down is called the AILERON. There are no rudder controls for turning the car to the right or left. In order to do this the driver must fire the side engines one at a time. (Firing the left jet will cause the car to turn right, and vice versa.)

flap that can be opened and closed manually. This is where the driver enters and exits his or her car.

The foot pedals—gas, brake, and clutch—are right to left, as in conventional street vehicles. The gearshift lever is floor-mounted. In Team Fastex cars, the starter is a button on the dashboard to the left of the steering wheel.

A jump lever located on the floor on the right side of the seat activates rockets for short jumps over opponents, crashes, obstacles, and holes in the road.

Each of the cars has a signature move and a signature move lever to control it. The signature move lever is a handle parallel with the windshield that is attached to the ceiling of the cab, where it can be easily reached by the driver's right hand. To activate it, the driver pulls it down. To deactivate it, the driver pushes it back toward the ceiling of the cab.

■ Signature Moves

On Charger's car, the signature move lever fires booster jets, which slide out from each side of his car and also blast from the undercarriage of the front of his car. The jets allow drivers to maneuver quickly.

On Flyer's car, the signature move lever makes delta wings pop out from the undercarriage sides of the car, and booster jets fire from the rear of his car. This allows Flyer to sail over cars ahead of him.

On Stunts's car, the signature move lever uses jets in the undercarriage to tilt the car up on two wheels on the same side, allowing it to pass another car or obstacle in a narrow space. The signature jets are strong enough to lift not only Stunts's car, but another as well. However, Stunts's signature move can be dangerous. If another car hits him while he is up on two wheels, his car may tumble out of control.

On Spitfire's car, the signature move lever deploys rockets, which expand from the sides of her car, increasing her speed considerably. Megan later redesigned her car so that her signature move became the firing of a single large rocket engine in the back of her car, which also increases her speed. The single rocket's advantage is that it is less likely than the side rockets to be shorn off or damaged in a collision.

■ Instruments and Gauges

All cars have both headlights and taillights for safety in

tunnels and during night races. Sensors in the roof of the car activate head- and taillights when the environment turns dark, as in a tunnel or at night.

Instruments and gauges are necessary to tell the driver how hot the engine is, how much gas is left, and other important facts about the car. Generally, instruments are circular. One of the gauges nearest the driver, just to the right of the steering wheel, displays the engine temperature. Under extreme conditions, a color bar at the top of the instrument flashes red. If nothing is done to reduce the engine's temperature, the glass over the instrument will crack. Another instrument is the tachometer. It reads the engine speed in revolutions per minute.

On the center console is an emergency button that can be used to shut down the engine under dangerous circumstances. However, if the heat sensors are disabled or a modified control chip is inserted, the new forced combustion carburetors could overheat, causing the throttle to stick in an open position. When the engine is in this extreme condition it cannot be shut down. Worse yet, the heat becomes critical long before the car runs out of fuel. As it reaches a critical condition, flames shoot out of the glowing red carburetor, indicating that the car is on the verge of exploding. All a driver can do at this point is downshift, steer the car clear of other drivers and spectators, and deploy the Rescue Racer. The driver must try to out-race the fireball caused by the explosion.

Because the cars go so fast in quickly changing situations and road conditions, it is very important that a driver be constantly aware of his or her surroundings. Therefore, Team Fastex cars have TV monitors rather than rearview mirrors. Using this feature, the driver can see what is behind, what is on either side, or even what is above his vehicle.

Every car is also equipped with a camera that records the actions of the driver. These records can be viewed later by the driver and other team members to observe what the driver does under certain circumstances.

EXTERIOR

The exterior designs of each Team Fastex car are slightly different, and each driver has his or her own personal paint scheme.

Charger's colors are red with yellow accents.

Spitfire's colors are purple with yellow and blue accents.

Stunts's colors are green with yellow and purple accents.

Flyer's colors are blue with white and yellow accents.

Many aspects of the Team Rexcor car interiors are similar to those of Team Fastex. Following are a few notable exceptions.

The dashboard of each Team Rexcor car is equipped with a video screen used to communicate with team owner Garner Rexton.

With a button on an array above the windshield, The Collector can open a small pair of sliding doors in the front side of his car and release a grappler, which has an arrow-like hook. When fired at another

car, the hook can cause an instant blowout in one of its tires. The Collector's car can then rush by the troubled vehicle.

Using a switch to the left above the windshield, The Collector can launch a small object like a

BLUEPRINT

MISC. ACTION BUTTONS
SIGNATURE MOVE LEVER
REAR VIEWER
TACHOMETER
STARTING BUTTON
STEERING WHEEL
OIL GUAGE
TEMPERATURE GUAGE
GEAR SHIFTER
JUMP LEVER
RESCUE RACER LEVER

Japanese throwing star from his front fender. This object is a scrambler. It is designed to fly across the open space between cars, attach itself to the target car, and—at the flick of another switch—cause the target car's computer to give an incorrect reading of an off-road racecourse. (A red light on the scrambler blinks when activated.) This has proven to be a very effective trick for Rexcor, as a driver often fails to notice that his or her computer is giving a false reading until he or she is so lost that he can never hope to catch

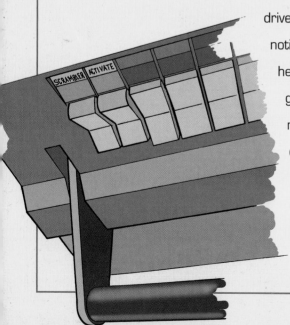

up. However, the information the scrambler gives may be so wrong (showing the driver on a course in San Diego rather than the Alaskan tundra, for example) that the driver will notice, and will therefore make corrections to the computer.

By flipping a switch just to the right of the shift lever, Junker can open a hatch on the hood of his car and fire a pair of grappling hooks. A lever resembling a hood release is under the dashboard. Pulling it causes one of Junker's own rear tires to blow. This forces his car to swerve across the track, making him an obstacle to the other cars in the race.

■ Signature Moves

The Team Rexcor signature move handles are identical to those of Team Fastex. However, the signature moves themselves are very different.

A driver's skill in deciding which tire tread to use in a given situation can be put to the ultimate test in the Motorsphere, where a variety of weather conditions can be artificially created. Rain, hail, sleet, and snow all call for different treads—and in the Motorsphere, these conditions can all be created within moments!

On The Collector's car, the signature move lever causes the back end of his car to fold open, revealing jet engines that rise into position on either side of the car's main body. This allows him to fly for short distances.

On Specter's car, the signature move lever slides open the rear panels of his car to reveal a single powerful rocket engine, which gives him a giant boost of speed.

On Junker's car, the signature move lever drops pieces of his car—fenders, bumpers, tail pipes, and so on—into the paths of other cars.

On Zorina's car, the signature move lever deploys a single rocket booster from the back of her car.

CAR SAFETY SYSTEMS

High speeds and complex machinery make NASCAR Unlimited Division racing a dangerous sport. For this reason, designers put a great deal of effort into making the cars as safe to drive as possible.

STRUCTURAL INTEGRITY

Cars and their suspension systems can withstand hard knocks, such as a bump from another car against its roof. (This can be a major concern in a racing division where many of the cars have airborne capabilities). However, if one car lands on

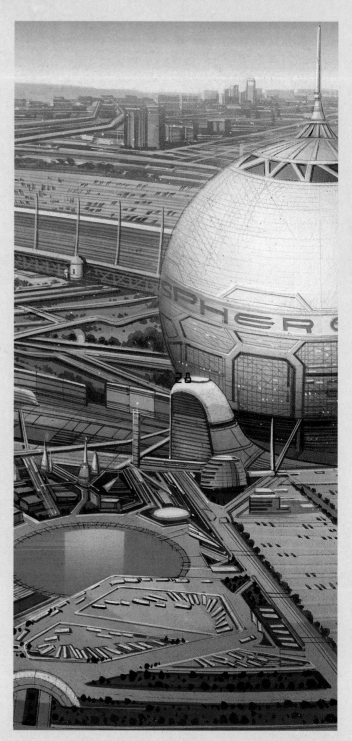

the roof of another too hard, the bottom car may suffer a cracked windshield.

DROGUE CHUTES

A drogue chute is a parachute that can be released from the rear of the car to help with braking. After use, it can be detached from the car. However, such an action can be dangerous to cars behind it because the chute can cover the following car's windshield. The chute can be used only once in a race.

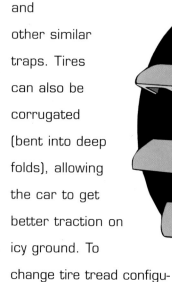

MORPHING TIRES

Conventional tires have a tread pattern which, except for normal wear, will not change over its lifetime. That is why morphing tires are more suited to Unlimited Division racing. Morphing tires can grow a special tread configuration on the driver's demand to match specific road conditions.

For example, a deeper tread may be useful for getting out of sandpits

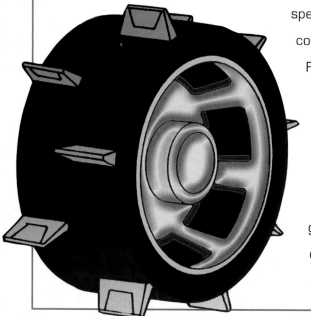

and other similar traps. Tires can also be corrugated (bent into deep folds), allowing the car to get better traction on icy ground. To change tire tread configuration, the driver need only push a button behind the signature move lever over the windshield.

Morphing tires are well-tested before use. Early tests in spike configuration showed that the tires dug up the track. On retraction, the test car flipped over. This was later corrected, and spikes can now successfully be used on muddy off-road courses.

Unlimited Division tires in their normal (unmorphed) state are made out of high-grade rubber, and will smoke against the track on jackrabbit starts and on sudden braking. The tires are very durable, but can be punctured by sharp objects.

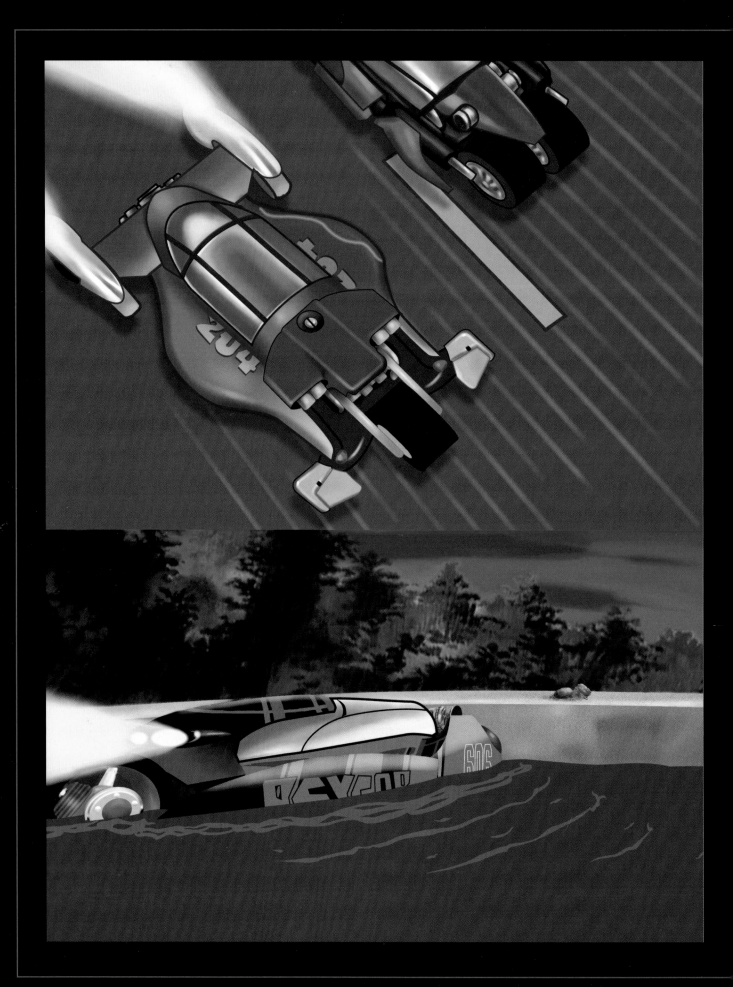

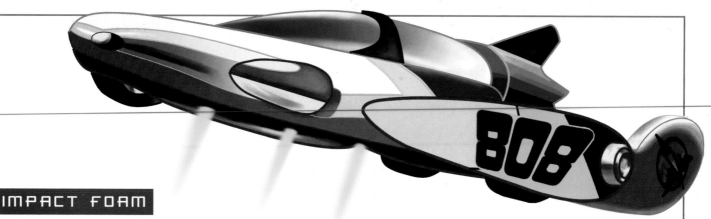

IMPACT FOAM

Deployment of *impact foam* is automatic, activated by crash sensors throughout the car. During a collision, the foam fills the driver's compartment, entering the cab through the hub of the steering wheel, through vents in the door, and from the cushion behind the driver's head. The foam becomes rigid instantly upon contact with the air, encasing the driver in a protective shell. Seconds after impact, the foam disintegrates, allowing the driver to exit his or her car or operate his or her Rescue Racer.

RESCUE RACERS

A Rescue Racer is an alternative to impact foam. It is a smaller ejection vehicle built into the main car. The unit is self-contained, with wheels and a small, separate engine. A driver can eject the Rescue Racer to avoid a collision, leaving the main car behind. If a driver uses a Rescue Racer during the last lap of a race, he or she may finish the race in it.

On Team Fastex cars, the handle to deploy the Rescue Racer is a bar on the dashboard. The bar is similar in design to the one above the windshield that controls the signature move. The driver pulls the bar down to arm explosive bolts, release couplings, and pop the car's canopy, instantly ejecting the Rescue Racer. If the Rescue Racer is released into the air, the driver pulls back a lever in the center console to deploy the wings.

Deploying the wings may sometimes flip the Rescue Racer over, so that it is flying upside down. If that happens, the driver may push a button on the main dashboard, firing booster jets—one above the wing, the other below—which can be used to flip the Rescue Racer over, so that it is right side up. The Rescue Racer is also equipped with impact foam, which deploys automatically under sufficiently critical conditions.

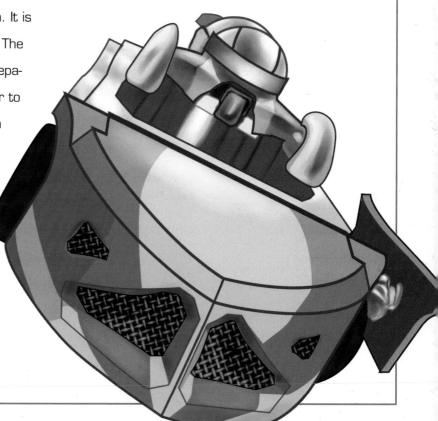

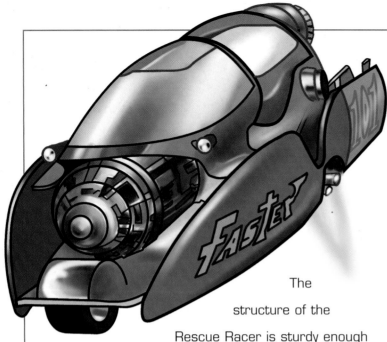

The structure of the Rescue Racer is sturdy enough to protect the driver however it hits the ground, right side up or upside down, but is not designed to handle every situation. For example, early Rescue Racers were not designed to float. However, while they were soon modified so that floating is now possible, they are still not very maneuverable in fast-moving water.

■ Team Fastex Rescue Racers

The design of each Rescue Racer is unique to the car in which it is contained. Team Fastex has some of the most interesting Rescue Racer designs in the Unlimited Division.

Charger's Rescue Racer has a rectangular air intake at the front. It has two small wheels in the front at the ends of outriggers, and one wheel in the back. Four exhaust pipes protrude from either side of the structure behind his head.

Stunts's Rescue Racer has two protected wheels in front, and a single wheel in back. It has a vertical rectangular air intake and a set of three exhaust tubes behind the cockpit.

Flyer's Rescue Racer has wings that are permanently deployed.

Spitfire's Rescue Racer has one protected wheel in front and two exhaust tubes on either side of the cockpit.

■ Team Rexcor Rescue Racers

The Collector's Rescue Racer is similar to a motorcycle, as it has one wheel in the front and one in the back. His shift lever is mounted on the steering column.

Zorina's Rescue Racer has a pair of front wheels with a side stance, and a single rear wheel.

Specter's Rescue Racer has three unprotected wheels, one in front and two in back.

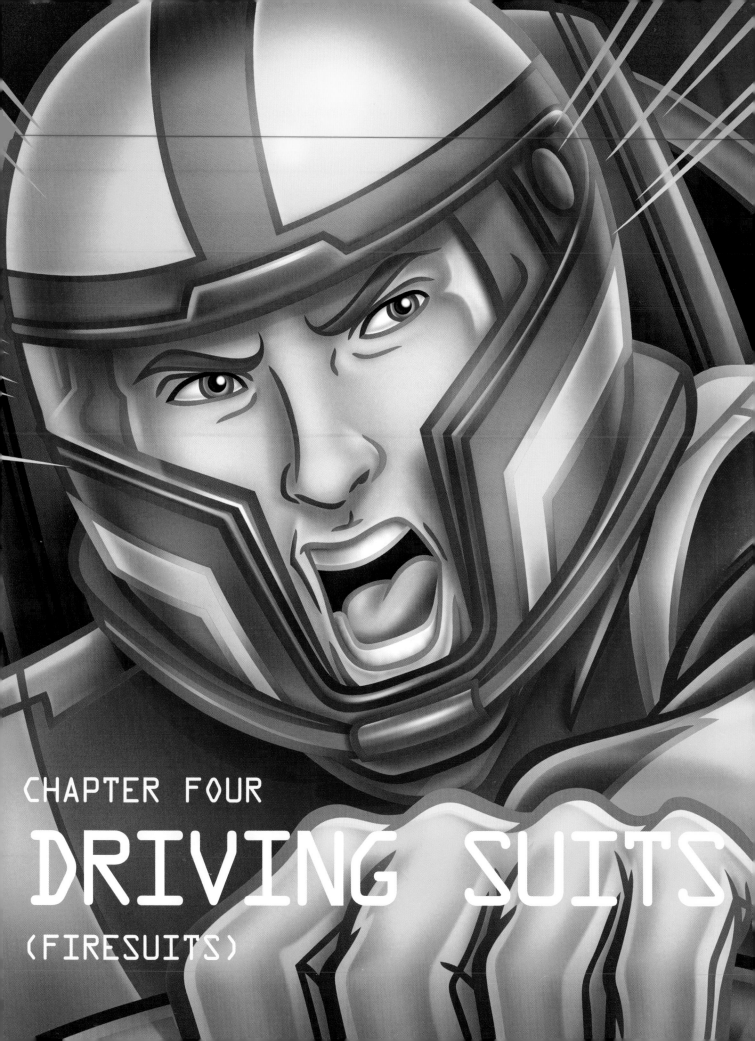

CHAPTER FOUR
DRIVING SUITS
(FIRESUITS)

A

DRIVER'S FIRST LINE OF DEFENSE against injury is his or her own intelligence and skill. After that, the driver must depend on his or her equipment, such as the Rescue Racer and the driving suit. Just as no two drivers are the same, no two driving suits are either. They are color coded, not only to promote individuality, but for easy identification.

How to Identify Team Fastex

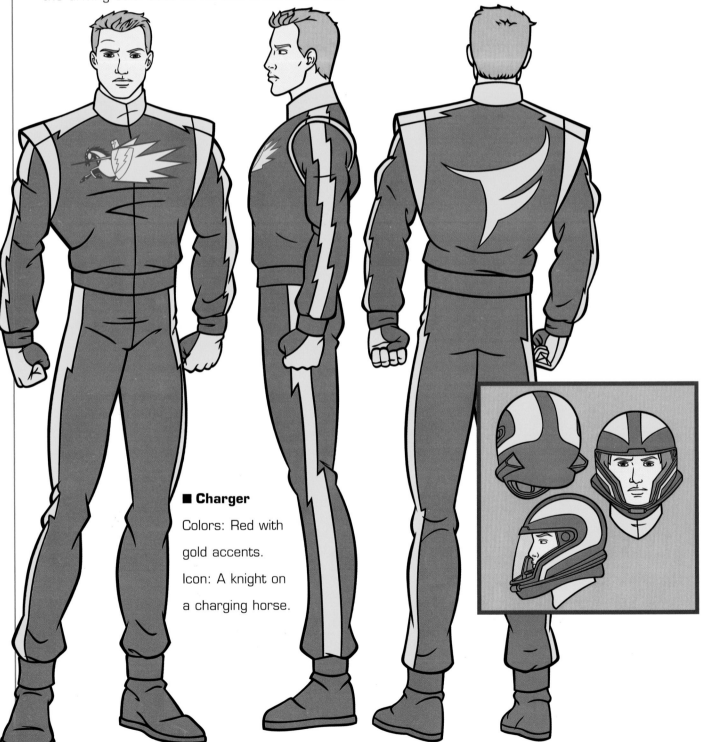

■ **Charger**

Colors: Red with gold accents.

Icon: A knight on a charging horse.

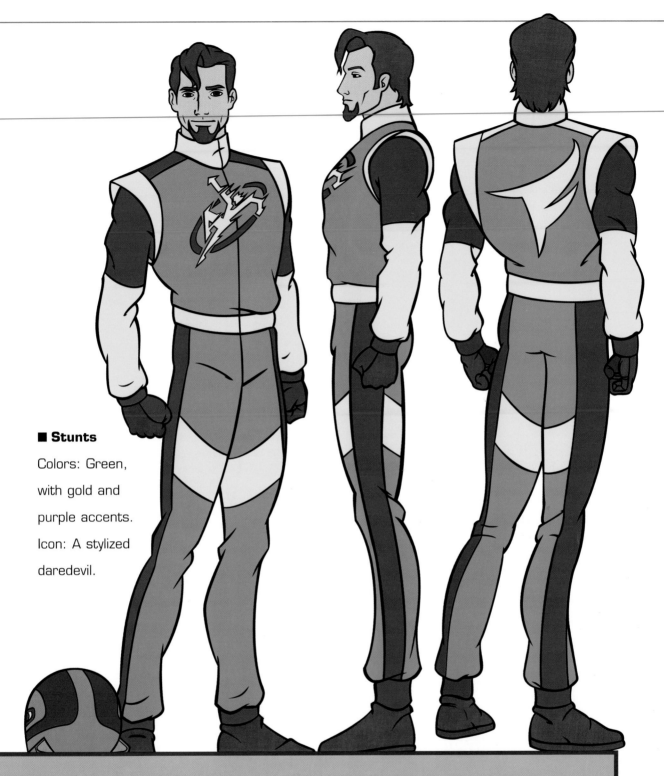

■ Stunts

Colors: Green,
with gold and
purple accents.
Icon: A stylized
daredevil.

All Unlimited Division helmets feature a foam core surrounded by a superstrong shell to cushion and protect the driver's skull. This durable housing also serves to protect the communications gear inside. It is vital that this gear remains in working order, especially during an off-road race, where a driver in a collision may well find him- or herself far off course.

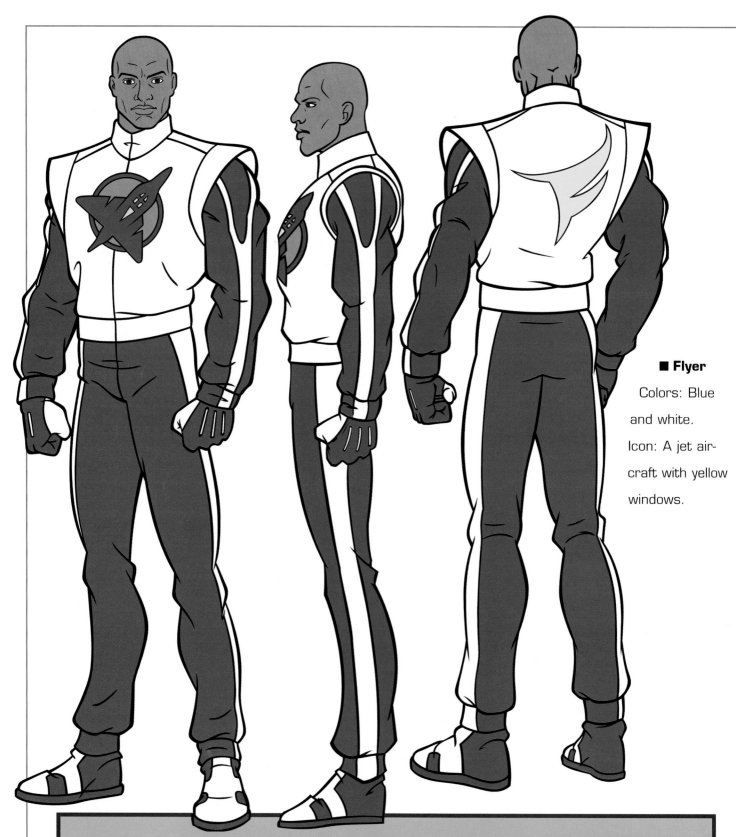

■ Flyer

Colors: Blue and white.

Icon: A jet aircraft with yellow windows.

Firesuits are made from an industrial-strength fabric developed for the Unlimited Division by Flexoco Gasoline. It is hoped that this flame-retardant, lightweight fabric will soon be available in protective gear manufactured for firemen.

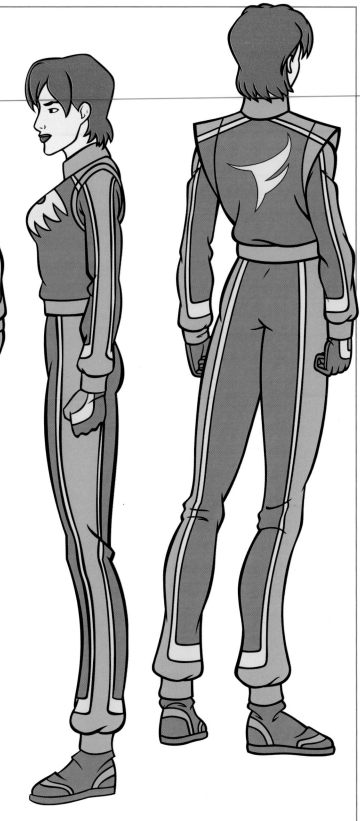

■ Spitfire

Colors: Purple, with blue and gold accents. Icon: A stylized bird of prey.

Capabilities:

Because driving suits are fire-resistant, they are sometimes called firesuits. Helmets are air-cooled and contain communications gear, with which drivers may talk to each other as well as to their pit crews. The radios in the driving helmets are independent from the racing car's other systems and can be used when the car is not even turned on. A driver may also speak to base using a small handheld auxiliary radio.

A strong swimmer may swim in his or her suit. The suits are well-insulated. After climbing from freezing water and walking around in deep snow, a Team Fastex driver will show no evidence of freezing. However, eventually, the cold will seep into even a Team Fastex firesuit.

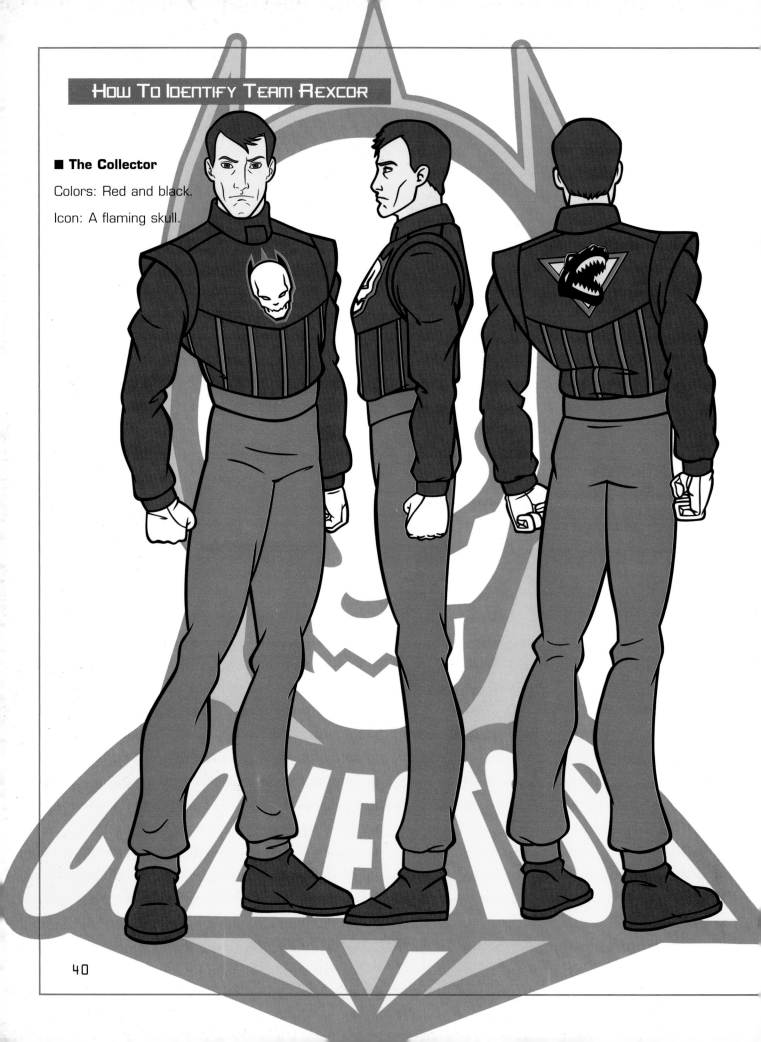

■ **The Collector**

Colors: Red and black.

Icon: A flaming skull.

CHAPTER FIVE
SUPPORT
VEHICLES

THOUGH THE RACING CARS ARE the vehicles that get the most attention, they are not the only important vehicles in Unlimited Division racing. Support vehicles also contribute to a super-car's ability to win a race.

IMP: The Independently Mobile Pit unit is a garage on wheels. The IMP accompanies a team to every race, whether it is off-road or speedway. For off-road races, the IMP moves at highway speeds while a racer refuels. A racing car can roll up onto the IMP from behind, or the IMP can scoop up a disabled car with its hydraulic front ramp. The IMP can do anything a stationary pit can do, including refueling, repairing, and changing tires using equipment stored in the "below-decks" storage compartments. Team Fastex and Team Rexcor employ at least three IMPs each. In the Team Fastex IMP, mechanical arms check tires and handle refueling. Duck usually sits in the "mechanic's seat," a seat at the end of a powerful mechanical arm that can quickly carry him to any point on the car.

Once adjustments to the supercar have been made, it can rejoin the race by driving off the IMP's front ramp. On speedway or short off-road courses, the IMP can be driven to the track and left in one place.

Tow Truck: This truck does what any tow truck is designed for (i.e. transporting injured vehicles from one point to another), but has been modified so that it is also fast enough to outrun an ordinary car or pull aside a hauler with its lifting hook.

Hauler: The hauler looks like an enormous tractor-trailer rig, but it can do things that no big rig ever could.

TEAM FASTEX HAULER

The hauler is as mobile as the IMP. It contains a driver's cab, a lounge and locker room for drivers and crew, a communications center, and emergency living quarters. It also carries equipment, tools, and spare parts. The team's racecars are carried in an overhead storage compartment.

The hauler's main room has one of the most advanced communications systems in the world. TV screens monitor races held inside the Motorsphere. The whole site is computer-controlled, and is

equipped with classic CD-ROM disk drives. The computers hold important information such as car specifications, team biographies, and track information from around the world.

Communications are facilitated by an antenna, which can be extended when the hauler reaches its destination. At the top of the antenna is a crow's nest or observation tower from which observers may get a live unobstructed view. The crow's nest contains two seats. Between them is a control cluster containing, among other things, a lever that hydraulically extends the tower many feet into the air. Once fully extended, the tower may sway a little in the breeze.

The ready room is a home away from home for the team, and contains everything a driver needs. The lockers have spring-loaded hangers, which help drivers change clothes in a hurry.

TEAM REXCOR HAULER

The Team Rexcor Hauler looks a lot like the Team Fastex model and has many of the same features. One difference is that it has a pair of rocket engines mounted on the roof near the back of the trailer. The tractor is designed to fold open, so that cars can be driven onto a second or third level.

One may climb a step or two and enter through double doors at the back of the rig. The first room contains spare tires, tools, and other equipment. A door at the other end of the room leads to the communications room.

The communications room is packed with radio receivers, radio transmitters, and other similar high-tech equipment. Video monitors are arrayed in a circle hanging from the center of the ceiling. A full size holographic image of a person or thing may be projected downward from the center of the video monitor array.

To the left as one enters are four video disk recording/playing machines, one that will concentrate on each Rexcor car during a race. Each VDR has its own monitor.

At Rexton's order, Spex may use the keyboard in his torso to raise a tower on the hauler. After the tower rises to its full height, a square housing at the top opens to reveal a microwave beam projector. At a command from Spex, the projector emits an invisible beam of concentrated microwaves onto a target, such as a car on the racetrack. Once the target is locked in, the projector fires the microwave beam, causing electronic disruption that looks like a natural short circuit. This causes the car to malfunction, ensuring that it is removed from competition.

CHAPTER SIX
RACING

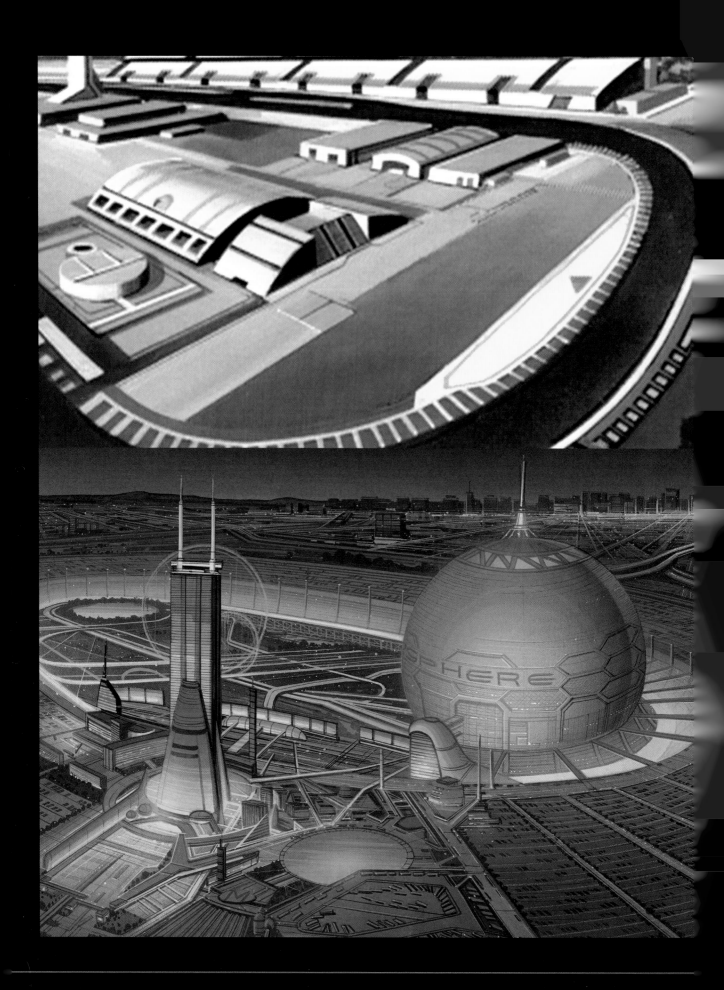

the fans, the cars, the drivers, the crew, and the track. The crew considers several factors about a track when planning a race. How is the track paved? How steeply banked are the curves? If the race is off-road, what is the terrain like? Special circumstances call for special plans—and special equipment.

SPEEDWAY RACES

Big River Raceway is the centerpiece of New Motor City, and the site of the first and last races of the Unlimited Division season. This complex of drag strips, speedways, parking areas, viewing stands, and garages is the final word in car racing architecture. Access roads allow drivers, crews, and raceway maintenance people to drive quickly and easily from one location to another. One can also turn off the main track onto the main access road. The infield track is skirted by a jogging track. In the center of the infield is an ornamental lake with a roadway over it.

■ The Track

Spotted around the entire track are computer-controlled cameras that record everything a Team Fastex car and driver do. Such records can be viewed later to help team members plan strategy and avoid making the same errors.

■ The Motorsphere

The Motorsphere is a challenging training ground, exciting in its own right, where the members of Team Fastex test their skills. Inside, a number of track and weather conditions may be artificially created.

Entry to the Motorsphere is through a short tunnel. Because the cars are able to go so fast inside the sphere, centrifugal force (a force that pulls objects outward when they go around a turn) allows them to race up the sidewalls and across the top of the sphere, where they race upside down!

Enormous screens on the inside surface show track action. Smaller spheres hang inside the main sphere; each one is a surface on which any product can be advertised.

■ The Pit

The pit area has almost one hundred bays extending down one side of the track. It has its own loading zone, where a hauler may pick up and drop off cars, and anything from a spark plug to a new engine may be delivered. The Team Fastex pit area is not to be confused with the Team Fastex garage, where even more complex operations may be done. Large screens over the pit area show what is happening on the track.

■ Team Fastex Garage

The Team Fastex garage is clean and well-stocked. Using its facilities one can do anything from

> The steepest bank on a regular **NASCAR** racing division track is 36 degrees. The steepest bank in the Unlimited Division is a mind-boggling 360 degrees—a full circle, where racers can drive upside-down! Without Unlimited Division forced-combustion technology and unparalleled safety systems, this sort of driving would be impossible.

change a tire to rebuild an engine. At the rear of the big room are a number of computer terminals for use by the drivers and crew.

TEAM REXCOR RACEWAY

■ Team Rexcor Garage

The Team Rexcor garages are similar to that of Team Fastex. However, one unique feature is the large turntables set into the midline of the garage floor. These are used to revolve cars so that they are held in just the right position for repair.

EXOTIC SPEEDWAY RACES

Unlimited Division races take place at exotic venues all over the world. Special equipment can be added for extreme off-road courses—sharp blades in jungles, or special tires for desert courses. Again, it is up to the crews and engineers to decide what equipment will be most useful for any given off-road race.

GLOBAL POSITIONING SYSTEM

The Desert 500 is run in a Spanish-speaking country called Secado (which means "dry" in Spanish). Teams Fastex and Rexcor also compete in the Tundra 2000, a race through the Alaskan prairie. Because of its cold, snow, and freezing road condi-

tions, the Tundra 2000 is known as one of the most grueling races on the Unlimited calendar. On such cross-country races there are checkpoints at various locations along the route to ensure the safety of the drivers. Each car carries a Global Positioning System that receives satellite signals telling the car where it is. An onboard computer map shows the car's location. It also shows team members aboard the hauler the locations of the various team cars. Such locating equipment is particularly useful when running off-road races through rugged, unfamiliar areas.

For the Tundra 2000, Team Fastex and Team Rexcor cars were outfitted with extra equipment useful for driving through harsh terrain during winter, including a snowplow and super-strong spikes on the morph-ing tires.

Off-road races are already conducted on the varying terrains of Alaska, Arizona, and South America. Use this map to mark the locations of new challenging terrains as they're discovered.

The snowplow attachment developed for Arctic conditions can shovel up to *four tons* of snow! This is useful for clearing paths in areas with heavy snowfall, and would even be strong enough to get a driver through a minor avalanche.

For any given race through dense forest area, cars are equipped with a double buzz saw—twin rotating circular blades, which can be used to cut down trees, thus clearing a path through a forest. The blades are at the ends of arms that come out from under the front of the car. The switch that deploys them is located on the left above the windshield.

A night run on a street circuit around Manhattan resulted in the creation of the most advanced shock absorbers in racing history. Because city streets are not as well cared for as formal tracks, this was of special importance to the driver's safety.

Engineers must make special adjustments to the forced-combustion system for races such as those run through the Andes Mountains. Here, high altitudes mean that little air can get into the engine. This decreases the engine's power. To make up for this, some crews added external super chargers to the engine to give the racer added thrust.

Unlimited Division engineers worked overtime to improve handling on the racers for the race on the Bonneville Salt Flats, which had the longest straightaway and highest speeds in NASCAR history. The drivers had to maintain control of their cars at speeds up to—and over— 400 miles per hour!

The midwinter race in St. Petersburg, Russia, that crosses frozen Lake Ladoga requires the latest in morphing-tire technology. Superslippery surfaces can be dangerous to drivers if they cannot get an adequate grip on the track.

A race across the Sahara Desert near the pyramids caused engineers untold trouble as they strove to keep sand out of the Unlimited Division engines. The final answer? A heat-resistant fine mesh covering the workings under the hood!

NASCAR Unlimited Division races through hot regions such as the Sahara pose special problems for the Division's high-heat forced-combustion carburetors. In these races, the cars have added cooling systems, not just for the drivers, but for the engines, as well!

CHAPTER SEVEN
TRAINING

SOME MEN AND WOMEN ARE BORN with the potential to be great drivers. But even they must hone, develop, and practice their skills in order to realize that potential. Training is very important. There are two kinds: live and virtual. While live training is useful, most Unlimited Division teams rely on virtual training. Virtual training offers a safe environment in which drivers can adjust their skills to the technical and design innovations of Unlimited Division vehicles. This is vital for their understanding of how the vehicles work.

The training simulator is usually used to simulate normal race conditions, but can also be used to test driver response in potentially life-threatening situations. Ultra high-speed racing requires microsecond response time, which can be greatly improved with practice and preparation on a simulator. Virtual training is far superior to live, because it allows the driver to prepare for any situation without actually placing the driver in physical danger.

BLUEPRINT

SIMFAS 4000

VIRTUAL TRAINING

Megan Fassler invented the Team Fastex training simulator, which realistically recreates the experience of Unlimited Division racing. The simulated view of the world outside is projected directly onto the training car's windows. Four trainers—one for each Team Fastex driver—are housed in the simulation room of the training building, T67. Each simulator is connected to a master computer by heavy cables that hang from the ceiling. The simulator computer accepts verbal commands given in the command center or in any of the simulators. Diagnostic functions can be initiated verbally, and the computer answers the same way.

The simulator can also reproduce emergency situations such as those requiring deployment of a Rescue Racer.

Observers can view what the drivers see in the simulations on screens in the command room. The screens can also be used to replay past simulations and access complete dossiers on drivers.

The Team Rexcor simulator functions in a similar manner to the Team Fastex model. One minor structural difference is the circular roll bar that arcs over the top of each Team Rexcor simulator unit.

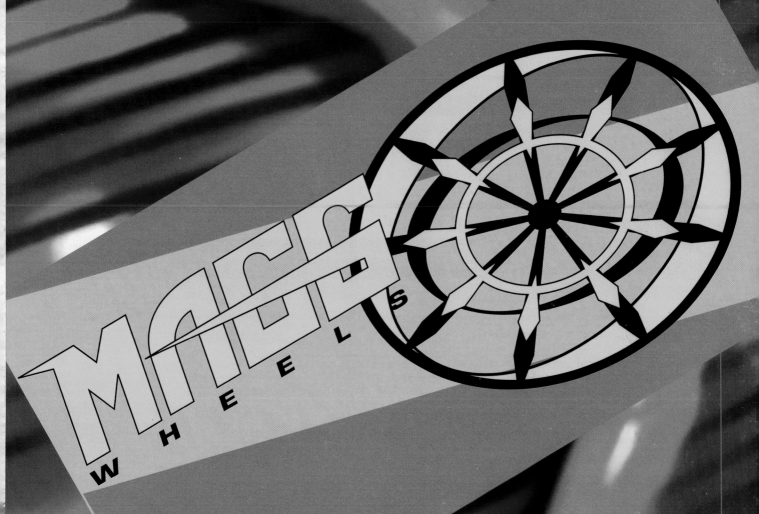

MAGS
WHEELS

CHAPTER EIGHT
SPONSORS

RACING IS AN EXPENSIVE SPORT. Building and maintaining cars, tracks, and facilities costs big money, and that is why corporate sponsors are very important. Some sponsors contribute not only funding, but technology as well. Flexoco Gasoline, in particular, has pioneered Unlimited Division research into high-octane fuel. And Greatyear Tires was instrumental in executing the morphing tire technology now employed on the racers.

Following are a few of the Unlimited Division's major sponsors:

GLOSSARY

HERE ARE SOME TERMS
YOU'LL HEAR AROUND THE RACETRACK.

car jockey: Someone who drives a car in a NASCAR race.

checkered flag: A flag that signals the end of a race. A symbol of victory.

cockpit: Also called the cab. The location in the car where the driver sits.

collected (in a crash): To be affected by a crash or other track disaster during a race.

draft: To hang so close to the car in front of you that the suction caused by its movement pulls you along. Or simply, to follow closely.

drogue chute: A parachute that can be deployed by a driver to help slow his or her car. Sometimes used to confuse drivers following too close behind.

enough car (to win): A general comment on a car's capabilities. For example: Does a driver have enough car to win a difficult race?

finding a ride: Getting a job with a particular team.

green flag: It appears on the screen at Big River Raceway to begin a race.

hauler: Large truck-like vehicle that is a home away from home for Unlimited drivers. It is used to carry Unlimited cars and their equipment to remote locations, and it can act as a base of operations.

IMP (Independently Mobile Pit): A traveling pit that can be driven to a remote racing location.

impact foam: Chemical foam that automatically deploys into the cab of an Unlimited car to protect the driver from a potentially dangerous situation. Following impact, the foam dissipates, allowing the driver to easily exit the vehicle.

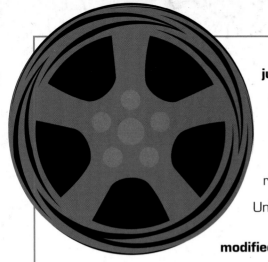

jump lever: Lever that activates booster rockets on the undercarriage or side of an Unlimited Division car.

modifieds: Cars that have been changed in some way.

morphing tires: Tires that can change tread patterns to match extreme road conditions such as dirt, snow, ice, or sand.

Motorsphere: Located in New Motor City, it is the largest and most sophisticated racing structure in the world. An enormous sphere in which drivers may experience a variety of racing conditions.

pit: The location where a car stops for maintenance during a race. Hence, the "pit stop."

position tower: A tall structure on which the lap number and other information is displayed to the fans during a race.

red flag: A red flag on the electronic flag board at Big River Raceway is a signal to stop the race. This may happen if the track becomes blocked or a condition exists that makes the race impossible to continue.

rescue racer: A small vehicle with an engine, contained inside an Unlimited Division car which ejects from the car in case of a life-threatening crash or track disaster.

ride, a: Employment. See "finding a ride."

rookie: A new driver.

signature move handle: Handle above and right of the driver on most Unlimited Division cars. It activates the signature move, deploying jets and wings specific to that driver and car.

simulator: A sophisticated, computer-controlled training device that is able to present drivers with a variety of racing conditions.

spoiler: A horizontal fin on the back of a car that helps stabilize it and keep it on the road.

spotter: A member of the maintenance crew who stands at some high vantage point and is in constant radio contact with the driver and his pit crew. He reports on road conditions, accidents, and other items of interest.

sprint cars: Small, fast-moving cars that are very hard on their tires, engines, and other parts, used for short races.

Unlimited Division: A new division of NASCAR comprised of cars equipped with futuristic designs and powerful new features.

yellow flag: When a yellow flag appears on a screen at Big River Raceway, it indicates that drivers should exercise caution, for example, if debris is on the track. Cars may not pass each other during a yellow flag condition.

The Unlimited Division is the future of auto racing.
These machines and their capabilities are experimental
right now, but they could soon become standard features on normal cars—perhaps even by the time you
have your driver's license! And remember, this division
will always need fearless drivers, engineers, and crews
to keep the machines humming—and the supercars
winning. From morphing tires to the forced-combustion
carburetor, the hauler to the IMP, from the off-road
race across the Sahara to the Motorsphere at Big
River Raceway, the possibilities for this division are

unlimited.

Join the NASCAR Racers winner's circle!

NASCAR RACERS

Enter to win this ULTRACOOL Sweepstakes!

One lucky Grand Prize Winner, along with his or her parent or legal guardian, will receive a FREE trip to the official NASCAR SpeedPark closest to his or her home!

TO ENTER: Send in a contest entry form located at the back of *NASCAR Racers #1: The Fast Lane; NASCAR Racers #2: Taking the Lead; NASCAR Racers: How They Work;* and *NASCAR Racers: Official Owner's Manual* OR send in a 3 X 5 card complete with your name, address, telephone number, and birthday to the address below:

Official Rules:

No Purchase Necessary to enter or win a prize. This sweepstakes is open to U.S. residents 18 years and under as of September 1, 2000, except employees and their families of HarperCollins Publishers, NASCAR, Saban Entertainment, and their agencies, affiliates, and subsidiaries. This sweepstakes begins on April 1, 2000 and all entries must be received on or before September 1, 2000. HarperCollins Publishers is not responsible for late, lost, incomplete, or misdirected mail. Winners will be selected in a random drawing on or about September 1, 2000 and notified by mail shortly thereafter. Odds of winning depend on number of entries received. All entries become property of HarperCollins Publishers and will not be returned or acknowledged. Entry constitutes permission to use the winner's name, hometown, and likeness for promotional purposes on behalf of HarperCollins Publishers. To claim prize, winners must sign an Affidavit of Eligibility, Assignment and release within 10 days of notification, or another winner will be chosen. One Grand Prize of a free trip to the NASCAR SpeedPark closest to the winner's home will be awarded (approximate retail value, $2,000). HarperCollins Publishers will provide the sweepstakes winner and one parent or legal guardian with round-trip coach air transportation from major airport nearest winner to the NASCAR Speedpark closest to the winner's home, 2-day passes into the NASCAR SpeedPark, and standard hotel accommodations for a two-night stay. Trip must be taken within one year from the date prize is awarded. Blackout dates and other restrictions may apply. All additional expenses are the responsibility of the prize winner. One entry per envelope. No facsimiles accepted.

Airline, hotel, and all other travel arrangements will be made by HarperCollins Publishers in its discretion. HarperCollins Publishers reserves the right to substitute a cash payment of $2,000 for the Grand Prize. Travel and use of hotel and NASCAR SpeedPark are at risk of winner and neither HarperCollins Publishers nor NASCAR SpeedPark assumes any liability.

Sweepstakes void where prohibited. Applicable taxes are the sole responsibility of the winners. Prizes are not transferable and there will be no substitutions of the prizes except at the discretion of HarperCollins Publishers. For the name of the Grand Prize winner, send a self-addressed stamped envelope by October 1, 2000 to HarperCollins Publishers at the address listed to the right. VT and WA residents may omit return postage.

ENTER THE NASCAR SWEEPSTAKES:

Mail this entry form along with the following information to:

HarperCollins Publishers
10 East 53rd Street
New York, NY 10022
Attn: Department LP

Name:_____
Address:_____
City:_____
State:_____ Zip:_____
Phone #:_____
Birthday:_____